Cornet Student

by Fred Weber and Major Herman Vincent

To The Student

This book, with the aid of a good teacher, is designed to help you bec_____ ____ on your instrument in a most enjoyable manner. It will take a reasonable amount of w_____ ___ practice on your part. If you do this, learning to play should be a valuable and pleasant expe____

To The Teacher

The Belwin "Student Instrumental Course" is the first and only complete course for private instruction of all band instruments. Like instruments may be taught in classes. Cornets, trombones, baritones and basses may be taught together. The course is designed to give the student a sound musical background and at the same time provide for the highest degree of interest and motivation. The entire course is correlated to the band oriented sequence.

To make the course both authoritative and practical, most books are co-authored by a national authority on each instrument in collaboration with Fred Weber, perhaps the most widely-known and accepted authority at the student level.

The Belwin "Student Instrumental Course" has three levels: elementary, intermediate, and advanced intermediate. Each level consists of a method and three correlating supplementary books. In addition, a duet book is available for Flute, Bb Clarinet, Eb Alto Sax, Bb Cornet and Trombone. The chart below shows the correlating books available with each part.

The Belwin "STUDENT INSTRUMENTAL COURSE" - A course for individual and class instruction of LIKE instruments, at three levels, for all band instruments.

EACH BOOK IS COMPLETE IN ITSELF BUT ALL BOOKS ARE CORRELATED WITH EACH OTHER

METHOD
"The Cornet Student"
For individual
or
brass class
instruction.

ALTHOUGH EACH BOOK CAN BE USED SEPARATELY, IDEALLY, ALL SUPPLEMENTARY BOOKS SHOULD BE USED AS COMPANION BOOKS WITH THE METHOD

STUDIES AND MELODIOUS ETUDES

Supplementary scales, warm-up and technical drills, musicianship studies and melody-like studies.

TUNES FOR TECHNIC

Technical type melodies, variations, and "famous passages" from musical literature — for the development of technical dexterity.

THE CORNET SOLOIST

Interesting and playable graded easy solo arrangements of famous and well-liked melodies. Also contains 2 Duets, and 1 Trio. Easy piano accompaniments.

DUETS FOR STUDENTS

Easy duet arrangements of familiar melodies for early ensemble experience.
Available for: Flute
　　　　　　　Bb Clarinet
　　　　　　　Alto Sax
　　　　　　　Bb Cornet
　　　　　　　Trombone

Elementary Fingering Chart

For Cornet And Trumpet

Cornet

Trumpet

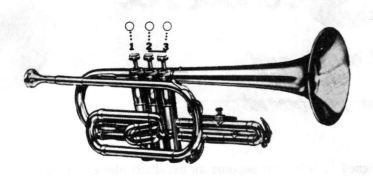
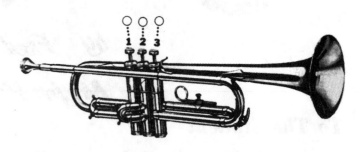

How To Read The Chart

● — means put valve down.

○ — means do <u>not</u> put valve down.

When two notes are given together on the chart (F♯ and G♭), they have the same sound and are played with the same fingering.

In order to make the fingering chart as easy to understand as possible, only those fingerings necessary in the elementary phase of Cornet playing are given.

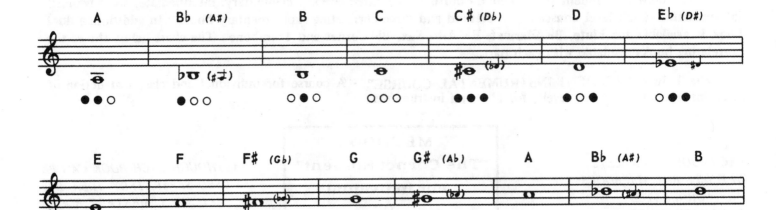

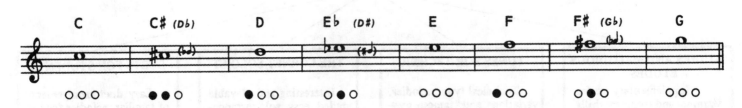

Getting Started

On the Cornet and Trumpet we can get several different tones without any valves by using different LIP positions.

FIRST DO THIS —
      Play any OPEN tone (NO VALVES DOWN). Hold it as long as COMFORTABLE and try to make it as CLEAR and STEADY as possible. Be sure the air goes through the horn in a steady stream.

      The tone you play will probably be one of THREE tones. We will call them "HIGH", "MIDDLE", and "LOW". Your teacher will tell you which one you are playing.

————————————————   **HIGH**

————————————————   **MIDDLE**

————————————————   **LOW**

High tones are easier for some beginners while others find the low tones easier to play. Omit the High note if difficult.

The note below is the MIDDLE tone from above.

The note below is the LOW tone from above.

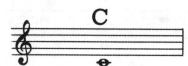

PRACTICE THE TWO NOTES ABOVE
      until you can play them with a steady and pleasant sounding tone.

WHEN YOU CAN PLAY THE TWO NOTES ABOVE
      try the notes below using the proper valves when necessary. MEMORIZE.

    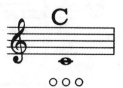

● – means valve down.   ○ – means valve up.

PLAY THE LINE BELOW.

      Hold each tone as long as comfortable, and be sure it sounds pretty and is clear and steady.

Lesson 1   Reading Music

You should know the following rudiments before starting to play:

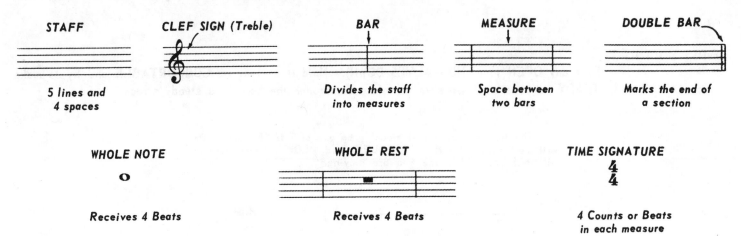

STAFF — 5 lines and 4 spaces

CLEF SIGN (Treble)

BAR — Divides the staff into measures

MEASURE — Space between two bars

DOUBLE BAR — Marks the end of a section

WHOLE NOTE — Receives 4 Beats

WHOLE REST — Receives 4 Beats

TIME SIGNATURE — 4/4 — 4 Counts or Beats in each measure

Notes and Musical Terms used for the first time are pointed out with ARROWS.
They should be memorized.

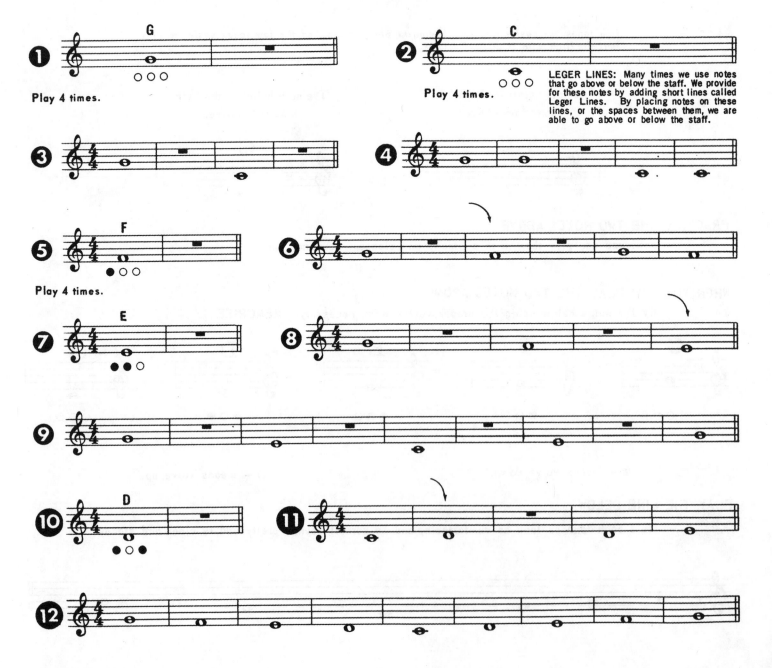

1 G — Play 4 times.

2 C — Play 4 times. — LEGER LINES: Many times we use notes that go above or below the staff. We provide for these notes by adding short lines called Leger Lines. By placing notes on these lines, or the spaces between them, we are able to go above or below the staff.

3

4

5 F — Play 4 times.

6

7 E

8

9

10 D

11

12

Lesson 2

Quarter Notes And Quarter Rests

QUARTER NOTE 1 count.

BREATH MARK - means to breathe.

For the first few pages, name and finger the notes before you play each line.

QUARTER REST 1 count.

Mary Had A Little Lamb

Put the NUMBER of the LINE or SPACE the note is on, in the square and write below whether the note is on a line or space.

Space

Lesson 3

PUT THE FOLLOWING ON THE STAFF:

Whole Note	Quarter Note	A Time Signature	Quarter Rest	Half Note	Half Rest	Tie two Notes

Lesson 4

You are now ready to begin the companion books, STUDIES AND MELODIOUS ETUDES and TUNES FOR TECHNIC, correlated with the Method as part of the BELWIN STUDENT INSTRUMENTAL COURSE.

HOLD Give extra time.

Work out carefully, then try for speed.

Hold each note as long as possible.

Tone must be steady.

DOTTED HALF NOTE Gets 3 counts.

TIME - 3 counts in each measure.

REPEAT DOTS - Play line twice.

Play 1st time only. Play 2nd time only.

--2nd time--

Lightly Row

Play 2 times. The first time play entire melody - second time, omit notes marked ★ and substitute a quarter rest.

Peter, Peter

A-Tiskit A-Taskit

PICK-UP NOTE (Ask your teacher to explain.)

Count 4 1 2 3 4

--2nd time--

Counting Fun   Duet

(Write counting under notes, then play.)

1 2 3 4 etc.

1 2 3 4 etc.

❶ Name the notes below. ❷ Indicate correct fingering.

The 1st one is done for you.

Name → E

Fingering →

Lesson 5

Lesson 6

Comparing C And ₵ Time

**① ** Same as 4/4

**② ** Means 2 Counts in each measure and 𝅗𝅥 gets ONE Count.

Jingle Bells

**③ ** Play 1st time only. Play 2nd time only.

This means the line may be played either in C or ₵ time. Practice the line in C time until you can play it well, then play the notes AT THE SAME SPEED but TAP in ₵ time (2 beats per measure).

The notes will sound the same, only the TAPPING will be different.

---2nd time---

**④ **

Counting Fun

Write counting under notes, then play.

**⑤ **

**⑥ ** * KEY SIGNATURE - means all Bs are played B♭ (See note below.)

**⑦ ** Notice   To remind you   1   2

Two Tune Duet

**⑧ ** 1st Part

2nd Part

Some people can play high notes sooner and easier than others. The C SCALE is first used in Lesson 8 on Page 12, however, a little exploratory practice on this scale might be helpful at this time.

Ask your teacher if he wants you to practice the scale below at this time.

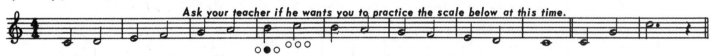

---

* Sometimes it is necessary to place a flat at the beginning of a line. This avoids the necessity of placing a flat in front of each B. When there is a flat in the signature it is always B♭ and the Key is F. It is in the Key of F because the melody, or study, is based on the scale of F.

Until No. 6 on this page there has been no Key Signature. When there is no Key Signature the piece is in the Key of C.

B.I.C.146

9

Lesson 7

Cuckoo Waltz

Repeat preceding measure.

Speed Drill

Play 4 times and work for speed.

Hold each note as long as possible.

Listen carefully to each tone.

A Skip Around Song

Count 3 1 2 3

Fine
(Finish)

D. C. al Fine
(Go Back to Beginning
and Play to Fine.)

Old MacDonald's Duet

Write counting under each line before playing.

Both lines played together as a Duet will sound the complete melody. One person can also play both lines for the melody.

On the staff below, write the note receiving the number of counts called for (in 4/4 time).

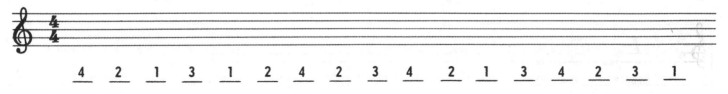

4 2 1 3 1 2 4 2 3 4 2 1 3 4 2 3 1

Our First Solo

On the top staff is a series of notes and rests. You are to rewrite this line on the bottom staff changing <u>notes</u> to <u>rests</u> of the same time value and <u>rests</u> to <u>notes</u> of the same time value.

Lesson 8

NEW NOTES

B♮ C

♮ NATURAL - cancels the effect of a Flat or Sharp.

To remind you the note isn't B♭

To remind you

March

To remind you

Speed Drill

Work out carefully then try for speed.

PICK UP NOTES

Marines Hymn

Count
3 4   1 2 3 4   1 2 3 4
2 +   1 + 2 +   1 + 2 +

Fine

D. C. al Fine

❶ Put in the Bar Lines.   ❷ Write counting under notes.

Lesson 9

This means gradually louder.

o scale.

LIP SLUR - A slur between two different notes *HAVING THE SAME FINGERING.*

Grandfathers Clock

Fine
(Finish)

D. C. al Fine

Caisson March

Write a **T** below the ties and an **S** below the slurs.

Lesson 10

You are now ready to play solos from THE CORNET SOLOIST, a book of solos with Piano Accompaniments correlated with the Method as part of the BELWIN STUDENT INSTRUMENTAL COURSE.

ACCENT MARK - play with force.

SIMILE - continue in a similar manner.

Intervals

Counting Fun

March

* See below.
2 Counts in each measure.

* *The second Flat does not concern you at this time. It will be explained later.*

FILL IN FINGERING and name note (B♭ or B♮).

REMEMBER - B♮ is plain B.

Lesson 11

#– A SHARPED NOTE—sounds ½ step higher.

Church Song

All Fs are played F#. The TOP LINE is also F.
  It is customary to put the sharp on this line when
  F is to be sharped. (The Low F is also sharped.)

No sharp

By comparing Numbers 2 and 5 it will be easy to see why we use Key Signatures at the beginning of a piece instead of putting
#s and ♭s before each note.

* See below.

Bicycle Built For Two

Double Note Duet

Student (or Teacher)

Teacher (or Student)

* When we have 1 sharp in the Key Signature it is always F# and the Key is G. It means the piece is based on the scale of G and all Fs are sharped.

Lesson 12

ALL Bs are played B♭ when there is one Flat in the Key Signature.

ALL Fs are played F♯ when there is one Sharp in the Key Signature.

Work out carefully - then try for speed.

Speed Drill

March Theme

Lesson 13

Eighth Notes

① Play Number 1 first in 4/4 time - then in Cut (¢) Time. Then play Number 2 as written. Compare Number 1 played in ¢ time with Number 2 played in eighth notes.

Your teacher will show you his favorite way of counting eighth notes.

③ If the foot-tapping method of counting is used make sure the foot comes UP (Up beat) in EXACTLY the MIDDLE of the BEAT.

Intervals

Play slowly and separate tones. **DO NOT STOP** tone with the tongue.

Chromatics

Also play slurred.

Skip To M'Lou

Melody Fun

Play 3 times. The first time play the entire melody. 2nd time - omit all notes marked with ✳ and substitute a rest.
3rd time - omit all notes marked ★ and + and substitute quarter rests.

① Name the notes. **②** Mark fingering.

Lesson 14

is intended to picture a well played tone that doesn't wave and stays on exactly the same pitch.
HOLD - Give extra time.

AVOID tones of the type pictured below.

ⓐ A "Scooped" attack. ⓑ A wavy Tone. ⓒ Attack not clean. ⓓ A Tone that goes flat. ⓔ (1) Accented tongue release. (2) Over-accented attack.

This Old Man

There's A Hole In The Bucket

When The Saints Go Marching In

Write the counting under the measures below.

Lesson 15

You are now ready for DUETS FOR STUDENTS, a book of easy duet arrangements of familiar melodies coordinated with the BELWIN STUDENT INSTRUMENTAL COURSE.

This means gradually softer.

LIP SLURS - Practice slurring two ways (*TOP* and *BOTTOM MARKINGS*).

Chromatics

Work out slowly, then try for speed.

Speed Drill

Billy Boy

Counting Fun
What tune is this study based on?

Lesson 16

Tune in KEY OF C (No Flats or Sharps)

1

Same Tune in KEY OF F (1 Flat)

2

Same Tune in KEY OF G (1 Sharp)

3

Scale Study in KEY OF C

4

Scale Study in KEY OF G

5

Scale Study in KEY OF F

6

Because You're You

7   C#

Grandfathers Clock

8   Count 2 1 2

Fine

D. C. al Fine

In the measures below is the second note HIGHER; LOWER; or the SAME as the first note? Use H, L, and S.

H

Lesson 17

1 *EIGHTH REST - same time value as eighth note (♪).*   *Staccato — means short or separated.*

etc.   etc.

NEVER stop the tone with the tongue.

2

Andante From Surprise Symphony
HAYDN

3

The Name Of This Key Is _____ ?
Work out carefully, then try for speed.

4

Swing High March

5 D#

Trio

Lesson 18

Work for a steady tone (as pictured) with no changes of pitch.

Enharmonic Tones

same sound

Intervals

simile

The Name Of This Key Is ___?

Work out carefully, then try for speed.

Mighty 'Lak A Rose

Lesson 19

1

Accent Mark
NEVER stop tone by putting tongue between teeth.

NOTICE - both ♩ and ♩ notes are separated.   ♩ is accented; ♩ is not accented.

2

simile

PATTERNS
Apply to Scale

ⓐ ⓑ ⓒ ⓓ

Speed Drill

3

SLUR 2 WAYS — as marked above and below.

Counting Fun

4

Mexican Clapping Song

5

The Blue Tail Fly

6

Lesson 20

1 Apply each pattern to entire scale in line 1.

PATTERNS ⓐ ⓑ ⓒ ⓓ

ff mf p

2 Eb (D#) Db (C#)   *same*   *same*

DOTTED QUARTER NOTE

3 The author suggests that you tap twice on the dotted quarter notes (♩.). The eighth note (♪) comes midway between the 2nd and 3rd taps.

America

4 *p* Stands for PIANO and means play softly.

5

Home On The Range

6 *f* Stands for FORTE and means play loudly.

Michael Row The Boat

7 Count 3 4 1 2 3 4

What KEY is this? _____   What KEY? _____   What KEY? _____

Lesson 21

A Page Of Counting Fun

Carnival Of Venice
Theme And Nine Variations

ALWAYS PLAY BOTTOM
NOTE ON REPEAT

TONGUING FUN - *Do not put tongue between the teeth.*

Lesson 22

1 Play staccato 1st time and legato 2nd time. (Legato means very smooth - use soft tongue stroke with NO separation of note.)

2 *When there are 2 Flats in the Key Signature — ALL Bs and Es are FLATTED.

4 Play tongued first, then play slurred as marked.

Work out carefully, then try for speed.
Speed Drill

College Song

6 *mp* — Stands for **MEZZO PIANO** and means to play moderately soft.

Over The Waves

7 *mf* — Stands for **MEZZO FORTE** and means to play moderately loud.
Same as Eb

Same as Bb

B.I.C.146

Lesson 23

Lip Slurs

Slur 2 ways.

Work out carefully, then try for speed.

Aura Lee

Name this KEY_____?

pp ← Stands for PIANISSIMO and means play very softly.

Band Boys March

ff ← Stands for FORTISSIMO and means play very loudly.

B.I.C.146

Lesson 24

The name of this KEY is_____?

1

The name of this KEY is_____?

2

The name of this KEY is_____?

3

The name of this KEY is_____?

4

Chromatic Review

5   **6**

7   **8**

9   **10**

Counting Review

11

12

Articulation Review

13

14

Lesson 25

1 ff f mp pp pp p f ff

2

3 See next line. ♪ - receives 1 Count.

4 ⅜ TIME - 3 counts to each measure.
KEY of_____ ♪ - 1 Count; ♩ - 2 Counts; ♩. - 3 Counts.

KEY of_____

5

The Man On The Flying Trapeze

6 mf

Sweet Betsy From Pike

7 mp   Same tempo ♪ = ♩   Don't stop

Lesson 26

Chromatic Scale

$\frac{6}{8}$ Time

$\frac{6}{8}$ Time is played exactly like $\frac{3}{8}$ Time except there are 6 Counts in each measure. (♩. = 6 Counts)

Glow Worm

ALWAYS check Key Signature and Time Signature before playing a line or piece.

America The Beautiful

Lesson 27

1 Also play slurred.

2 Separate each note. *simile*

3

My Wild Irish Rose

4 *p*

Yankee Doodle Boy

5 *ff*

Lesson 28

Sixteenth Notes

If the foot-tapping method of counting is used make sure the foot comes UP (Up beat) in EXACTLY the MIDDLE of the BEAT.

Jig

Bill Bailey, Won't You Please Come Home

Lesson 29

William Tell Theme

Variations On Skip To M'Lou

American Patrol

Lesson 30

Use 1 and 3 valves.

Bugle Call

Play using different valves and combinations (1st valve throughout, etc.).

Lesson 31

KEY SIGNATURE (See note below.)

Apply these patterns to Scale.

Scale Waltz

Circle all sharped notes.

Gypsy Love Song

p

Fine

D.C. al Fine

Turkish March

Barbara Allen

1 Name notes. 2 Mark fingering.

* When there are 2 Sharps, the second sharp is always C# and the Key is D. This means the piece is based on the D Scale and all Fs and Cs are sharped. The name of the Key is always the same as the line or space 1 note (½ step) higher than the last sharp in the signature.

Lesson 32

KEY SIGNATURE — See note below.

Apply these rhythms to the Scale.

Circle all flatted notes.

Brahms Lullaby

PHRASE MARK — Discuss phrasing with your teacher.

Play smoothly in a singing style.

* When there are three flats, the third flat is always A♭ and the Key is E♭. This means the piece is based on the E♭ Scale and all Bs, Es and As are flatted.

Basic Technic

Practice as assigned by your Teacher

Basic Technic
Lip Slurs

Basic Technic

Practice as assigned by your Teacher

The Patterns below provide for unlimited scale practice in the 7 most common band keys.

FOLLOW THESE INSTRUCTIONS.

Start with ANY line and play through the entire pattern without stopping. Return to the STARTING LINE and play to where the END is marked. You must keep the KEY SIGNATURE of the STARTING LINE THROUGHOUT the entire pattern.

Chromatics

Also play slurred.

Also play slurred.

Speed Test

Name the notes. Work for speed. Each test should be completed in 1 minute and 30 seconds or less. When completed turn the page upside down and try again.

Completed in _____ Seconds.

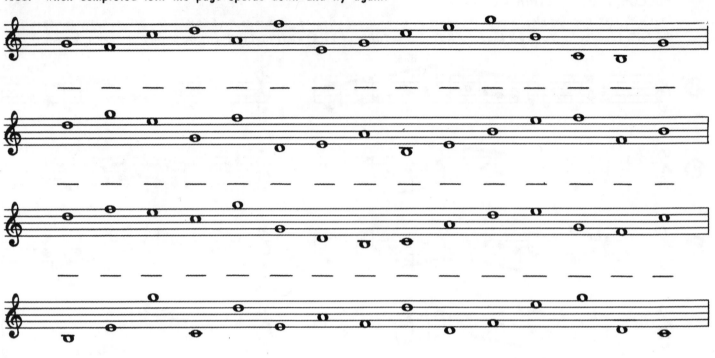

Home Practice Record

Week	Mon.	Tues.	Wed.	Thurs.	Fri.	Sat.	Total	Parent's Signature	Week	Mon.	Tues.	Wed.	Thurs.	Fri.	Sat.	Total	Parent's Signature
1									21								
2									22								
3									23								
4									24								
5									25								
6									26								
7									27								
8									28								
9									29								
10									30								
11									31								
12									32								
13									33								
14									34								
15									35								
16									36								
17									37								
18									38								
19									39								
20									40								